MW01248137

ISBN - Paperback: 978-1-06702-491-8

This book is dedicated to someone who proved to me just how strong a bond can be.

Emma Walker

Flash backs

They are constant,
some so traumatic,
and some sweet memories
of you.

They come in the day, and
swoop in during the dark of
the night.

So many flashbacks, but none
of them bring you back.

Hold me

Please hold me,
don't let me go.
Don't leave me alone.
keep me company,
I don't feel sound.

Don't leave the room,
I need you around.

Stress

Body, mind, spirit and soul,
so stressed, so on edge,
Where do I turn?
Where do I go?
This pain is so much,
how to cope,
I just don't know.

Rainy face

Rain from the sky,
rain from my eyes,
rain marks the pain
that my human
did not survive.

Grief tissues
1000 ply

Emma Walker

Next

The next breath,
the next step,
the next hour,
the next meal.

Breaking the day down,
when as a whole,
it's all too much.

Too hard to speak

Spring loaded

Your grief,
with you in every step.
like a spring gaining tension.

If you try to step away,
distract or take a breath,
the further you go,
the bigger the rebound,

All these emotions feeling like
they will drop you to the
ground.

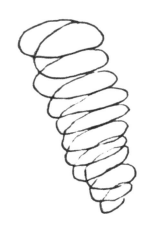

Hurts like hell

Having to cope when there's no
choice.
Having to try and establish a
routine of some sort,
whilst asking yourself,
What really is the point?

Feeding your body,
showering,
chores,
errands,
doing them all with your mind
somewhere else.

It's with the person you feel
like you can't live without.

Lonely

The loneliness,
Like solitary confinement in
your head,
fighting your own thoughts,
thoughts while alone,
alone in your thoughts.

The world keeps spinning,
you've spun out.
Spinning in your own world,
just you and your heavy heart.

Having to keep taking steps
forward when you never know
where to start.

You never know where to start
without completely falling
apart.

Emma Walker

Changes

Eating without hunger,
sleeping without rest,
driving with no destination,
conversations without meaning,
phone calls you don't answer,
bathtubs with cold water.

Nothing is the same.
I am forever changed.

Mornings

Rousing from sleep,
the weather is bleak,
to match my mind,
the internal forecast
holds no reprieve.

Things are hard,
things are rough,
I want you back,
my dearest love.

Jigsaw puzzle

The   life   I   had   envisioned
shattered into pieces.
pieces spread out everywhere,
they don't fit together,
pieces of my heart spilling out
all over the floor.

Too hard to speak

Into the forest

Heart shaped leaves,
gravel under foot.
off again I go,
feeling like a horse without a
hoof.

I take my grief with me, we walk
amongst the trees,
not taking much notice of the
gentle autumn breeze.

Emma Walker

Carparks

In the car parks I cry.
nobody notices or if so, they
don't ask why.

Pulling up to places,
but can't go inside.

I sit here and weep,
unable to speak,
reality feels so very bleak.

Photos

Please don't take photos of me.
I don't recognise myself.
Eyes full of pain,
I   can't   crack   a   smile.
If you ask me to do so,
it feels like a lie,
how can I smile,
My best friend did not survive.

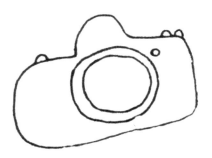

Books

I buy and I buy,
recommendations I must try.

They sit on the shelf,
I can't pick them up,
unable to read them,
but I know they may help.

Brain is foggy,
unsure of what to do.
All I can do is sit and think
of you.

Appreciation

For those that are there,
I appreciate you.

I know you care,
and I care about you too.
I truly do.

I just can't do much
to show you right now,
just how much
I appreciate you,
I wholesomely do.

Emma Walker

Unconditional

You keep showing up
through the rain and the pain
I appreciate you,
I truly do.

You haven't given up
and for that I am so grateful,
to have you in my life,
I'm undoubtedly thankful.

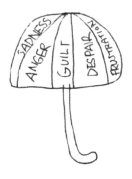

Language

Just like there are different
love languages, there are
different grief languages.

You are learning which one you
speak every day.
Learning which one those around
you speak too.

Often it feels so hard to know
what to say.

How do you comfort yourself,
let alone anyone else?

Emma Walker

Needs

Life is a muddle,
life is a blur,
everything so raw,
feeling so hurt.

Confused by messages
asking what I need,
I can't answer that,
I don't know what I need,
apart from my loved one,
But you can't bring them back.

Gentle

It is so hard to be gentle to
yourself when nothing about
grief itself feels gentle.

The universe has not been
gentle.

You are shaken to your core,
crushed by your loss.

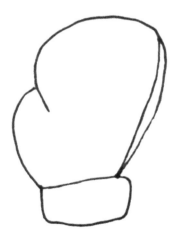

Emma Walker

Sundown

The sun ducks behind the line
of the horizon,
Its shadow sparks the desperate
sense of loneliness that
evenings bring.

Evenings spent staring out at
the stars, casting my mind back
to moments with you.

Moments I want back,
moments I need back.

Nightfall

Evenings represent a darkness
in the sky,
and darkness in my mind.

The darkness doesn't rise with
the sun.
There's no switch to turn it
off.

The darkness came the moment
you were gone.

This marks the moment my world
stood still.

Atlas

The atlas that I knew fell off
its axis.
my mind is spinning in the
opposite direction,
whilst the rest of the world
spins as it always has.

Nothing is as it always was.
nothing at all.

Everything has changed, and it
will never be the same.

This love, this grief will be
with me wherever I go.

Too hard to speak

Pulse rises

Mind racing,
when I see familiar faces
how they will react to me.
I'm not who I once was.
I never will be again.

I get by on adrenalin these
days,
body in fight or flight mode,
always feeling ready to
implode.

Determined to show up,
to try,
on my way there will be tears,
out in public I'm all bottled
up.

Everyday

Every day is difficult,
every day in pain.

Sometimes it shows on my face,
Sometimes you can hear it in my
voice,

Other days it's in my tears.
the tears that steal my voice.
other days, it's in my absence.

Absence from routine,
absence from conversation,
absence from the present.

I am not present,
I'm yearning for my loved one,
that's where you'll find me.

Too hard to speak

Pain

The pain of every day since the
moment you were taken away.
it's too much,
devastating,
completely earth shaking.

Heart is broken into pieces,
it can't be mended,
it's beyond repair.

The fact that I'm still here
without you here is too much to
bear.

My sweet angel, I need you
here.

Emma Walker

Basket

I carry my basket with me
everywhere I go.
It's filled with grief and
often overflows.
I try to pick up the pieces but
my basket tips and more spills
out.
I can't add more things to my
basket,
Grief has filled it up.

Overwhelmed and out of space,
I realise I am this basket.

This grief is part of me,
And it signifies a lot of love.

Lava

Blood as thick as maple syrup,
As hot as molten lava,
Flowing through my veins,
and then it reaches my heart.
It causes searing pain,
not physical pain.
It's emotion and its intense,

It keeps pulsing through my
body,
around and around again.

Emma Walker

People

All around they go,
about their days,
about their lives,
always on the go.

They're too busy to reply,
Although not too busy to post.

I'll protect myself over here,
and shy away like a ghost.

Too hard to speak

Carry

Where is the calm,
I fear it has gone,
so full of stress,
and less capacity to cope.

Unable to sit still,
but still not sure where to go.

It's not here,
nor there,
there's nowhere to go.

The pain comes with me,
We are one.

Joined together,
always together,
It's a part of me.

Emma Walker

No more

I can't do normal things
anymore,
at least not in a normal way.

The future I had envisioned has
been cruelly ripped away.

My brain has blunders,
It forgets and gets fogged.

It's not present in the moment,
It sits back in the past.

Anxiety

Another day of restless
anxiety, struggling to do
anything.
to make decisions or think
ahead is surely not a thing.

This is debilitating,
this is raw,
This is more than I can handle.

There really is no choice
though as I have been put in
this saddle.

Emma Walker

Places

There are places I can go,
But many that I can't.

Some I can go near,
but with others I stay far.

Some I went with you,
and others I only dreamed of.

Now I must go there without
you,
but my darling I will take you
right within my heart.

Hot element

Starting the day,
the temperature is palpable,
and once I get up,
the dial is turning,
temperature rising,
my heart is burning.

The stimuli,
the encounters,
the memories,
the triggers,

All ingredients to stir up,
my aching broken heart.

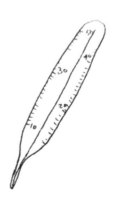

Expectations

Please lower your expectations,
I put enough on myself,
I'm not sure if you realize,
Just how much I'm hurting these
days.

It's not your job to fix this,
there really is no cure,
I just need lower expectations,
that much I know for sure.

Too hard to speak

Brave

I tell others they are brave,
Why do I not feel this way
myself?

I just feel so broken,
not brave,
not strong,
and not able.

Do others share these feelings?

I may never know,
most things aren't shared,
They're kept private,
A community of grievers tucked
away in silence.

Emma Walker

Changing tides

Changes of mood,
floods of emotion,
they come so quick,
like a rapid change of tide,
from the moon if it were
hyperactive.

Mother nature has a rhythm,
I have lost mine,
That I know.

I watch hers and wonder,
How she can be so steady and
slow.

Too hard to speak

Strong

Trying to be strong
through all the seasons.

The seasons of sadness,
of anger,
of guilt,
of despair,
and frustration.

There are many more seasons of
grief   than   there   are   in
weather.

The strange thing is that in
the thick of a grief wave,
you do just that,
You sit and you weather.

Emma Walker

Return

How do I return to what was,
there is not much left,
not much at all.

There is no way forward,
Nor one back either.

I stay here,
every single day,
until I find my words,
until I am strong enough for
change.

Too hard to speak

Hyperfocus

What once helped me to cope,
is now a survival skill.
I never knew I was training
myself.
for how impossible this is.

I have heard this before,
we turn to what we know,
to help ourselves through,
to try and return our flow.

Even with these things,
I still break and I stumble,
I keep falling and crawling.

I will just keep going,
I must,
there's no other way,
There's nothing in the world
that can take this pain away.

Emma Walker

Movement

Away from the flock,
I fly through the clouds,
Feeling that I am on the
bumpiest,
most uncharted path.

I separated from the rest,
the day I lost you,
this journey is solo,
that much I've learnt.

I think I'm still learning,
or maybe I'm stuck,
I've lost my compass.
and everyone just keeps flying
past.

Valid

These feelings are valid,
I know that they are,
but some can't be shared
with those I don't know.

My reactions to the triggers,
so real and so true,
I can't tell the person,
nor ask them to move.

They remind me of what I've
lost,
of whom got taken away,
triggers feel like a test,
but they're relentless,
they're all around,
for what feels like all day.

Turning

Twisting and turning,
In sleep,
and in wake.

Making decisions,
trying not to renege.

Mind always wandering,
trying to find its way,
whilst navigating being stuck
in a constant state of shock.

Too hard to speak

Healing

What does this look like,
How do I access it?

What do I do,
assuming where all different,
in our approach.

It's a broad term,
that much is obvious.

How do I know what I need,
when I'm struggling to exist.

Showing up

I think I am trying,
for those around me.

I'm not sure though,
as I don't feel myself.

Do they feel let down,
Do they notice I've changed.

Can they see I'm trying,
or do they not see me at all...

Too hard to speak

To do list

Is there a big list,
or is it not much,
I can't really tell,
but it feels like a lot.

Maybe I'm productive,
although it feels like I'm not.

I see others doing more,
I can't help but compare,
I have a lot on my plate,
It's hard to do less,
but I need more self-care.

Talk

Please talk of my loved one,
Please mention their name.
I need to share memories of
them,
They are all I have.

If you don't know what to say,
just admit that,
Its brave,
It allows me to start the
conversation,
to show you it's ok to speak.

Speak their name,
ask about them,
please do.
When you show an interest in
them,
I feel that much closer to you,
It's true.

Crowds

I thought I had friends,
I thought I had a crowd,
some of them have gone now,
I may not find out exactly why.

maybe they were never there,
Maybe the friendship was a lie.

With grief comes loss,
loss of a loved one,
loss of self,
loss of future,
and loss of health

You also lose friends,
other people in your life.
but you can't lose sleep over
those who chose not to stand by
your side.

Emma Walker

Shades

In shades of colour I look for
you,
in the sky,
in the ocean,
in objects,
some manufactured and others
nature made.

I will keep looking,
everywhere I go.

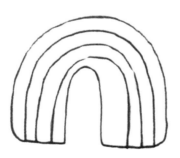

Activities

What type,
where do I go,
what do I do,
I'm struggling to know.

Through grief and trauma,
our habits change,
our interests change,
(or disappear).

Questions

When people say how are you,
do they really want to know the
truth,
maybe some do, and I'm sure
others don't.

How do I answer them,
What should I say?

What if I speak my truth,
and they don't stay,
or know what to say.

Road trips

Road trips used to be fun,
they used to be relaxing,
now they stir up the grief,
I listen to the songs,
sad songs,
but beautiful words.

Sitting in traffic,
starting to feel distressed,
do I turn around,
or stay in this lane.

Everyone is going in one
direction,
and here I am feeling alone,
travelling completely against
the grain.

Emma Walker

Whirlpool

Whirlpools of sadness,
potholes of despair,
sinking in anxiety,
reminded of the trauma.

Mind going on tangents,
circling on repeat,
like riding on a carousel.

Too hard to speak

Tomorrow

What will it bring,
how will I feel,
what do I tackle,
what do I not.

One day at a time,
the only way it seems,
each day different,
each day trying to figure out
where to start with my tired
aching feet.

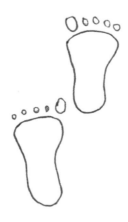

Winding up

Resilience isn't guaranteed,
grief changes you,
in so many ways.

You may be more stressed,
you may be less tolerant,
you may be less capable,
and struggle so much day to
day.

The resilience may come,
or it may not,
for now,
just focus on the fact,
that you're dealing with one
heck of a lot.

Too hard to speak

Stuck

Stuck in my thoughts,
unsure of where to turn,
am I better to distract,
or sit and face the facts.

Neither is easy,
Neither feels right.

My mind is facing the fight of
its life.

Emma Walker

Today

The thoughts were hard,
from first light of day,
They stung and they struck.

I sat with them sometimes,
Other times I had to move.
It's hard to stay still and
face the pain,
It's too much for me to do.

At times lighter,
Then heavier,
Then somewhere in between.

Another day of tumultuous
feelings,
another day of pain.

Home

I'm safe here,
from   triggers   and   unwanted
comments.
I can hide here,
focus on arts and craft.

It is lonely here,
but it is safe,
environment is controlled,
there's less anxiety.

Come visit me at home,
I will wait your company,
I know those who want to be here
will show up at the doorstep.

Company

I may not say so much,
or feel comfortable to speak,
or you might find me talking
in your company.

I never know how I will react,
or what my needs may be.

Every interaction different,
there's no guarantees.

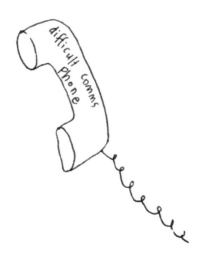